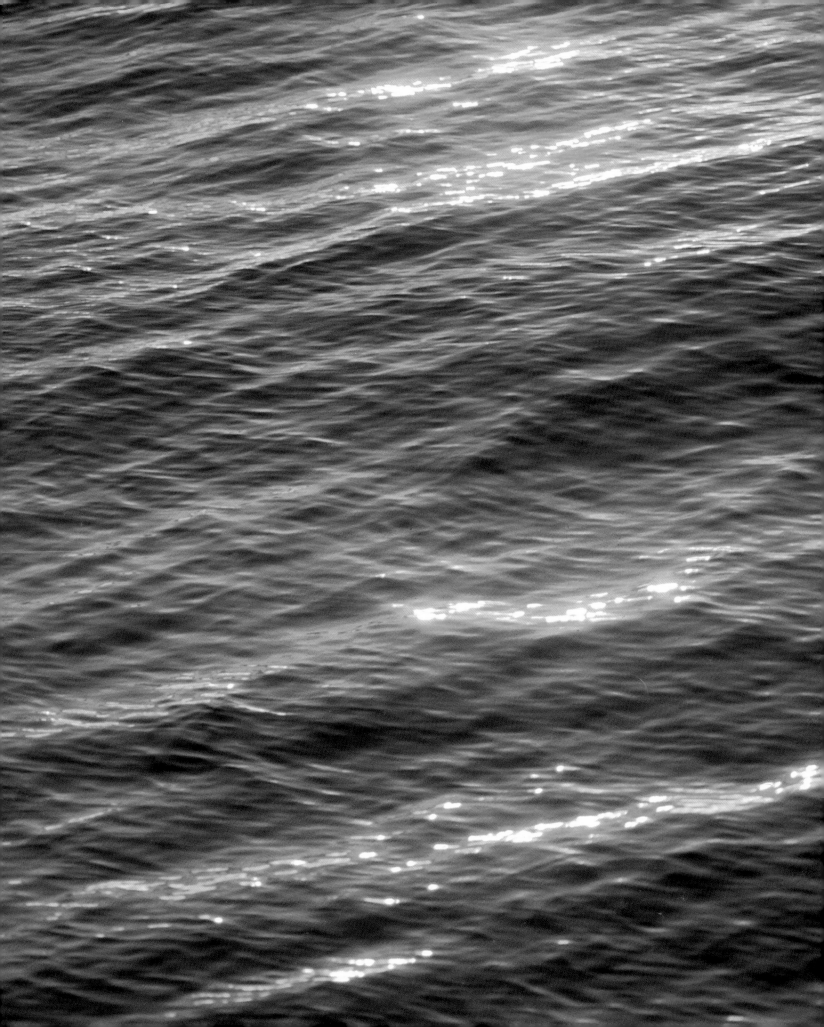

# WATER

## Jenny Markert

CREATIVE EDUCATION

Designed by Rita Marshall
with the help of Thomas Lawton

Photography by
Brian & Cherry Alexander,
Peter Arnold, Frank Balthis,
Tom Bean, Gary Braasch,
Michele Burgess, Bruce Coleman,
Jeff Foott, Mark Gibson,
George Huey, Llewellyn,
Les Manevitz, Ancil Nance,
NASA, Will & Angie Rumpf,
Jay Simon, Starlight,
Vaud Ancil Travis, and
Weatherstock

Library of Congress
Cataloging-in-Publication Data

Markert, Jenny, 1964–
Water / by Jenny Markert.
    p.   cm.
Summary: Describes water and the
essential characteristics it contributes
to life on earth.
ISBN 0-88682-431-1
1. Water—Juvenile literature.
[1. Water.]
I. Title.                    91-11641
QC920.G46   1991           CIP
551.46—dc20                  AC

*We live in a universe that is sprinkled with* trillions upon trillions of stars. One of these stars, the Sun, is circled by nine planets. Eight of these planets are lonely worlds. Some are extremely hot, others are extremely cold, but all are barren and probably void of life.

*Many worlds in the universe.*

The other planet that circles the Sun is remarkably different. Seen from space, this planet is colored a brilliant blue. On its surface, vegetation grows thick and green and creatures crawl, large and small. The planet is alive with sounds, colors, and activity. This living world, the only one in the Solar System, is our own planet Earth.

The Earth owes its uniqueness, in part, to a remarkable substance called *Water*. It is contained most obviously in the world's oceans. However, an intricate network of water also covers the Earth's land masses. Water lies frozen in glaciers, floats as clouds, and falls as rain. Water fills swamps and lakes, trickles down brooks and streams, and rushes down rivers and waterfalls. Water even hides in places never seen, buried in the soil and rock beneath our feet.

*Blue Earth seen from space.*

The total amount of water on the Earth does not change from day to day, or from year to year. However, water constantly changes from one form to another, and moves from one place to another. This never-ending movement of water is called the *Water Cycle*. Because of the water cycle, some of the water that you drink today could be the same water that a dinosaur drank 65 million years ago.

In order to understand how the water cycle works, we must imagine a drop of water with the tiniest dimensions. If you could divide a drop of water in half, divide the two halves in half, and so on, a thousand times, the bit of water left would be far too small to be seen, even under a microscope. However, that bit of water would contain millions of tiny particles, called *Water Molecules*. It takes billions of water molecules to make up a single drop of water.

*Rain clouds.*

Despite its calm appearance, a drop of water is never still. Every drop of water contains a small amount of heat. This heat causes water molecules to move. In every drop of water, molecules are speeding up, down, and all around. If two molecules collide, they bounce off each other and keep right on going.

When a drop of water is heated, its molecules begin to move faster. The fastest molecules actually break free from the other molecules and sail into the air. This process is called *Evaporation*. The free-flying water molecules, too tiny to be seen, form an invisible gas called *Water Vapor*.

*Breaking waves.*
*Inset: Dewdrops.*

14

Water vapor is always entering the air, because water is always evaporating. Water evaporates on hot, sunny days and on cold, cloudy nights. It evaporates from wet swimsuits, puddles, rivers, lakes, and oceans. Water also evaporates from the surfaces of plants, animals, and people.

Once in the air, water molecules are carried by the wind, sometimes for thousands of miles. On their journeys through the atmosphere, the invisible molecules often encounter changes in temperature. Whenever the temperature drops, the free-flying water molecules slow down. If the temperature drops low enough, the molecules slow down so much that they join together, or condense, into tiny droplets of liquid water. These water droplets are so small and light that they remain floating in the air. When countless numbers of water droplets collect in the air, they become thick enough to form a cloud.

*Condensation over a pond.*

When conditions are right, the tiny water droplets in a cloud combine to form larger drops of water. Gradually growing in size, the drops of water can become too heavy to remain floating in the air. When this happens, water falls out of the cloud as *Precipitation*.

*Rippling water.*

The type of precipitation that reaches the ground depends on the temperature of the air. When the temperature is warm, precipitation falls as small drops of drizzle or larger drops of rain. When the temperature is colder, rain mixes with ice to produce sleet. If the temperature is below freezing, precipitation falls as flakes of snow.

*Newly fallen snow.*

In many regions of the world, precipitation falls most often in the form of rain. Some of this rainwater soaks into the ground and collects in tiny spaces between rocks and soil. This hidden supply of water, called *Groundwater*, is pulled downward by the Earth's gravity. It flows downhill into rivers and lakes and eventually returns to the sea.

At times when rain is plentiful, all the spaces in the ground fill with water. The ground becomes saturated, and cannot hold any more water. When precipitation cannot soak into the ground, water collects on the Earth's surface. It fills small brooks and streams, accumulates in swamps and marshes, and collects in lakes and reservoirs. Pulled by the force of gravity, this water slowly travels downhill, combining into larger and larger rivers. Eventually, the flowing water makes its way back to the ocean.

*Surface water.*

21

As water weaves its way downhill, it wears away, or erodes, soil and rocks bit by bit. The water carries tiny pieces of this debris all the way to the ocean. Given enough time, water can wear down entire mountains and transform continents. The Colorado River is a dramatic example of the power of flowing water. For about two million years, this mighty river has gradually eaten into the Earth's surface. The majestic Grand Canyon is the result of this *Erosion.*

*Erosion in Utah.*

As we have learned, water is in constant motion. Water evaporates from lakes, rivers, and oceans in the form of free-flying water molecules. Sometimes, these molecules condense into clouds. And occasionally, clouds release precipitation. We have seen what happens to precipitation that falls as rain. What happens to precipitation that falls as snow?

During cold winter months, snow blankets the ground in many regions of the Earth. When spring comes and the days grow warmer, most of this snow melts. Like rainwater, the melted snow combines into streams and rivers and eventually flows back to the sea.

*Snow blankets the ground.*

In some areas, however, temperatures never rise high enough to melt the winter's snow. In polar regions and atop high mountains, fresh snow piles up year after year. Compressed by the tremendous weight of the accumulating snow, the lowest layers gradually change into solid ice.

Surprisingly, the sheets of ice that cover the Earth's polar regions and highest mountains do not remain motionless. Just as gravity pulls a skier downhill, it also pulls these masses of ice downward. These rivers of ice, called *Glaciers*, act like gigantic bulldozers, slowly plowing through rock and soil. Glaciers have carved some of the most stunning scenery on Earth.

*Glaciers.*

Though glacial ice seems to be a permanent state for water, it, too, is part of the water cycle. Glaciers that lie atop high mountains eventually flow past the snow line. There, they meet warmer temperatures, and slowly melt. The water then combines into brooks and streams and flows back to the ocean.

*Meltwater eventually flows to the ocean.*
*Inset: A thawing glacier.*

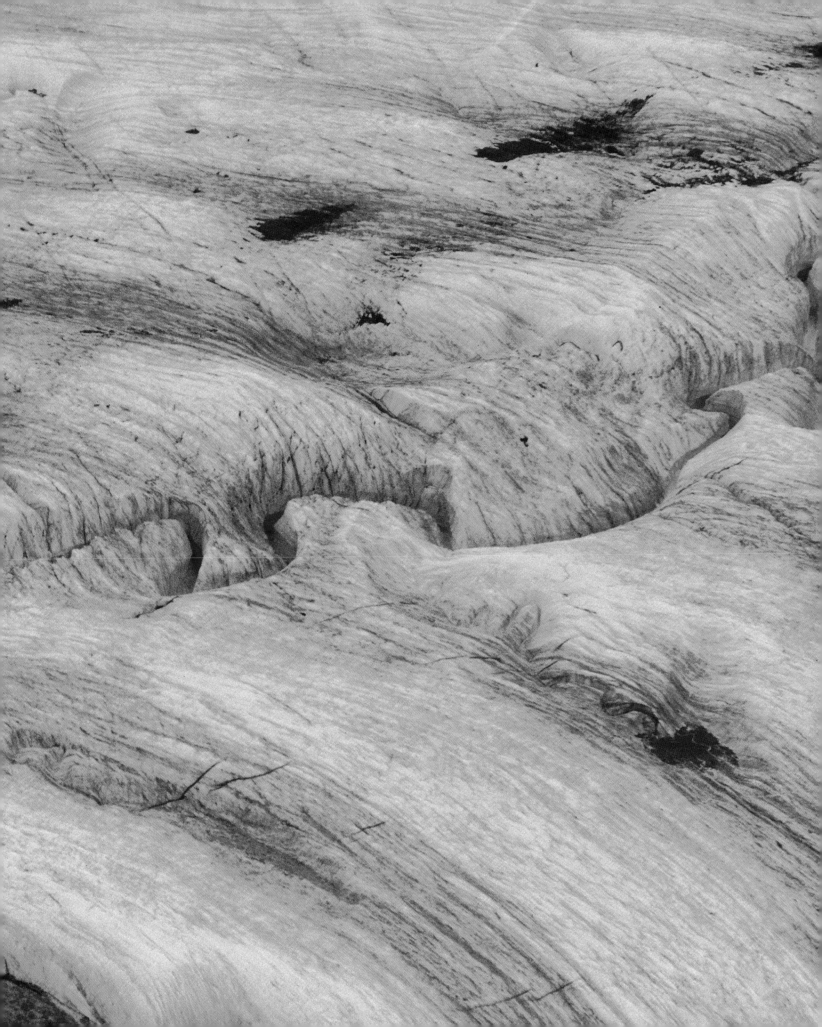

29

Unlike most mountain glaciers, glaciers in polar regions sometimes flow all the way to the sea. This is because temperatures in polar regions rarely rise high enough to melt the rivers of ice. When these glaciers meet a coastline, they are slowly chiseled by ocean waves. Gigantic slabs of ice break off the glaciers and float out to sea as *Icebergs*. Whittled by sunshine and warm ocean currents, the icebergs gradually melt and the water finally returns to the sea.

The fact that icebergs float is probably not surprising. Everyone knows that ice cubes float in a glass of water. However, this fact reveals an unusual property of water, one that makes our planet a pleasant place to live.

*Icebergs.*

Most substances contract when they cool. When water freezes, however, its individual molecules spread apart. The molecules in ice take up more room than the same number of molecules in liquid water. In other words, when water freezes, it expands. As a result, ice is lighter than water and therefore icebergs float.

This unusual, though familiar, property of water has important consequences. Because ice floats, it forms on the surfaces of lakes and oceans during cold winter months. When spring comes, temperatures rise and the ice quickly melts.

*The formation of ice crystals.*

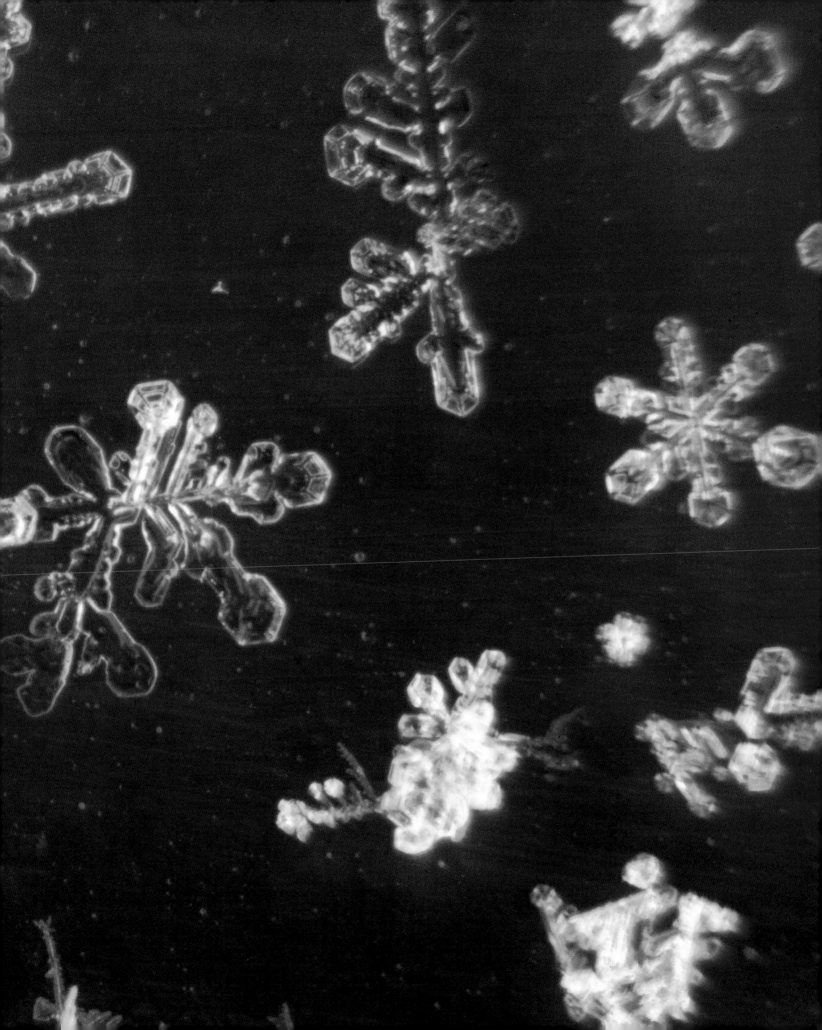

If water contracted when it froze, like most other substances, ice would sink rather than float. If ice sank, the Earth would be a very different world. Each winter, more and more ice would pile up on the bottoms of lakes, rivers, and oceans. Covered by water, the ice would not melt even during the warm summer months. Eventually, all of the Earth's water would turn to ice. Our planet would become a lifeless, frozen desert.

Water has other special properties that help make the Earth a comfortable place to live. Compared to most other materials, water changes temperature very slowly. If you have ever walked barefoot on a sidewalk on a hot summer day, you have probably experienced this property of water firsthand. The dry pavement may be scorchingly hot, while a nearby puddle remains relatively cool.

*Melting ice over a brook.*

The fact that water changes temperature relatively slowly has a dramatic effect on the Earth's climate. On planets where there is no water, temperatures vary between two extremes—searing heat and freezing cold. On the Moon, for example, the temperature during the day soars to over two hundred degrees Fahrenheit, and at night it may plummet to four hundred degrees below zero. Living organisms, including human beings, would have a difficult time surviving such extreme changes in temperature.

*An arid climate.*
*Inset: Desert plants are specially adapted to harsh conditions.*

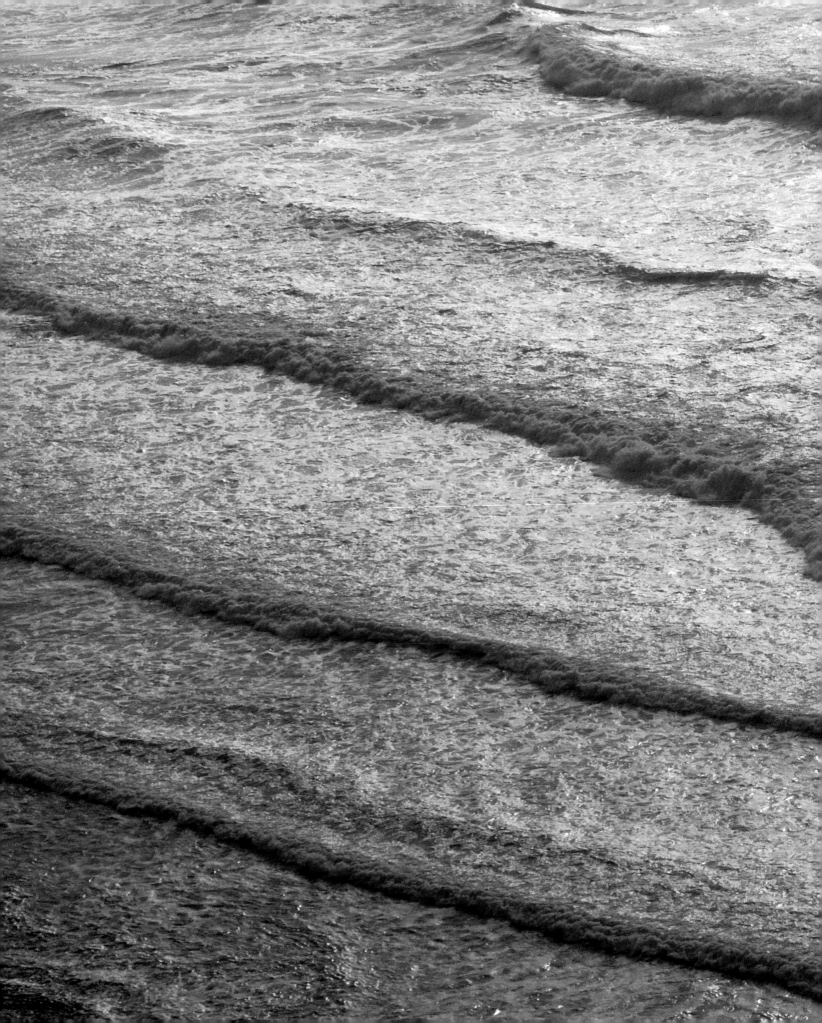

Fortunately, oceans cover about 70 percent of the Earth's surface. Since water does not change temperature easily, the ocean stays at about the same temperature all day long. The relatively constant temperature of the ocean, in turn, helps moderate the temperature of the rest of the planet. During the day, the ocean prevents the Earth from becoming extremely hot, and at night, it prevents the Earth from becoming extremely cold. Thus, the ocean keeps temperatures on Earth in the relatively narrow range that is necessary for life.

*Oceans cover most of our planet's surface.*

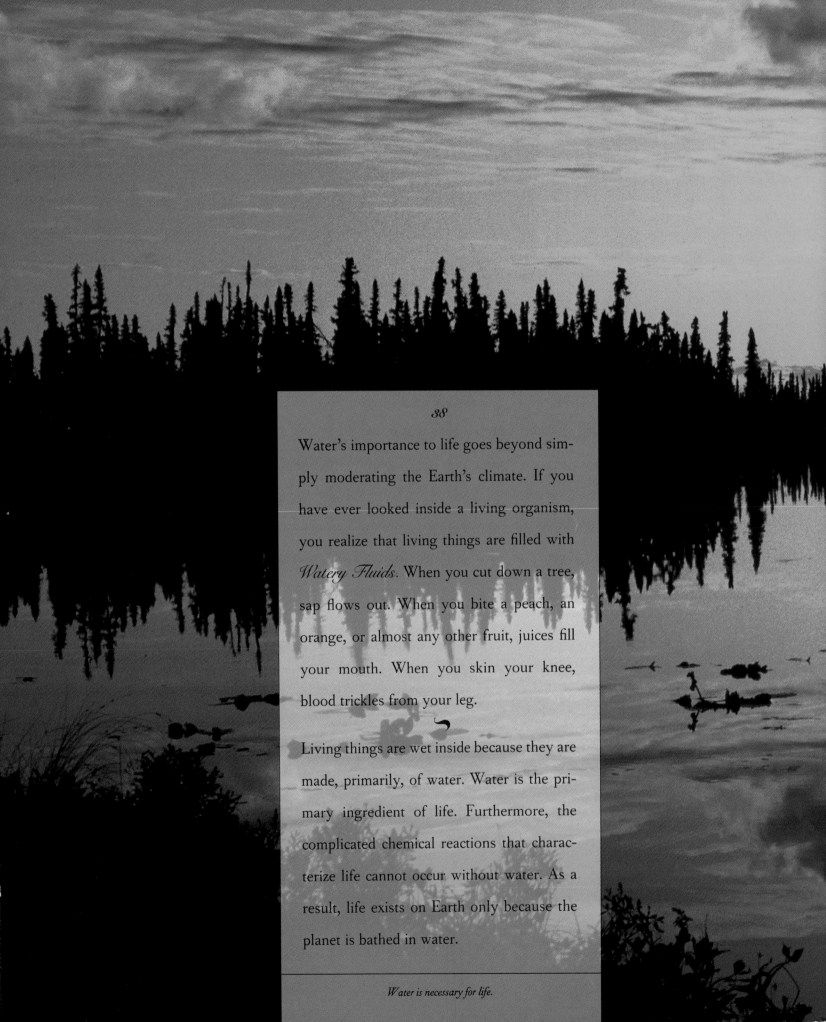

Water's importance to life goes beyond simply moderating the Earth's climate. If you have ever looked inside a living organism, you realize that living things are filled with *Watery Fluids*. When you cut down a tree, sap flows out. When you bite a peach, an orange, or almost any other fruit, juices fill your mouth. When you skin your knee, blood trickles from your leg.

Living things are wet inside because they are made, primarily, of water. Water is the primary ingredient of life. Furthermore, the complicated chemical reactions that characterize life cannot occur without water. As a result, life exists on Earth only because the planet is bathed in water.

*Water is necessary for life.*

Our living planet owes its splendor to the remarkable workings of *Water*. The water that covers our planet in the forms of mighty oceans, frozen glaciers, and flowing rivers makes the world a beautiful place. It carves channels, gouges canyons, and wears down mountains. Water fills our lakes, floats through our skies as clouds, and blankets our mountains as snow. But water does more than create beautiful scenery. With its unusual properties, water makes the Earth a unique haven for life.

*The never-ending water cycle.*